# Celtic Woman
## SONGS FROM THE HEART

**Alfred**

Produced by
Alfred Music Publishing Co., Inc.
P.O. Box 10003
Van Nuys, CA 91410-0003
alfred.com

Printed in USA.

ISBN-10: 0-7390-6720-6
ISBN-13: 978-0-7390-6720-8

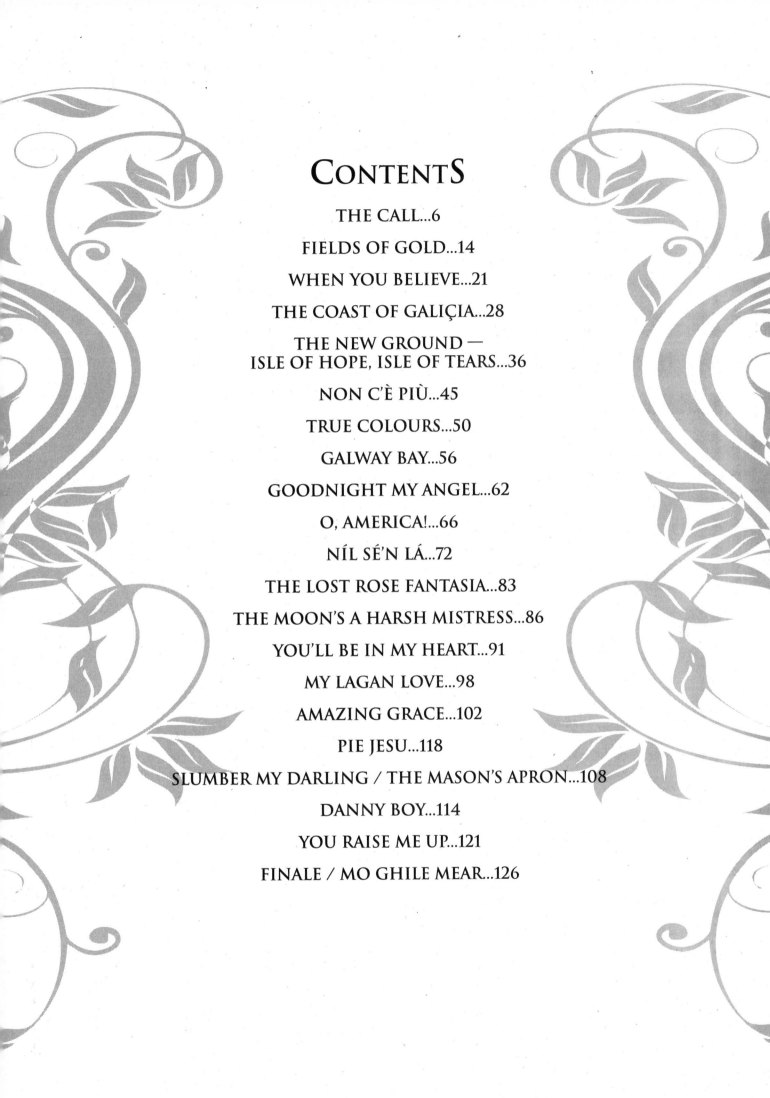

# CONTENTS

THE CALL...6

FIELDS OF GOLD...14

WHEN YOU BELIEVE...21

THE COAST OF GALIÇIA...28

THE NEW GROUND —
ISLE OF HOPE, ISLE OF TEARS...36

NON C'È PIÙ...45

TRUE COLOURS...50

GALWAY BAY...56

GOODNIGHT MY ANGEL...62

O, AMERICA!...66

NÍL SÉ'N LÁ...72

THE LOST ROSE FANTASIA...83

THE MOON'S A HARSH MISTRESS...86

YOU'LL BE IN MY HEART...91

MY LAGAN LOVE...98

AMAZING GRACE...102

PIE JESU...118

SLUMBER MY DARLING / THE MASON'S APRON...108

DANNY BOY...114

YOU RAISE ME UP...121

FINALE / MO GHILE MEAR...126

# THE CALL

Words and Music by
DAVID DOWNES and BRENDAN GRAHAM

*Verse 1:*

# FIELDS OF GOLD

Music and Lyrics by
STING

**Slowly, hauntingly**

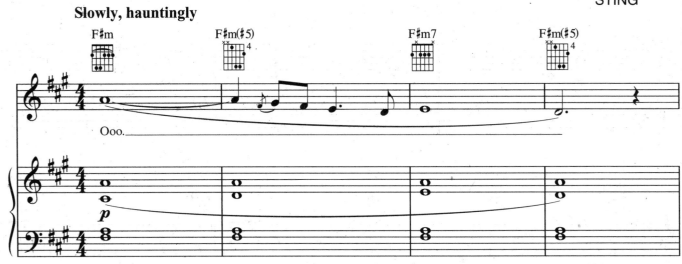

Ooo.

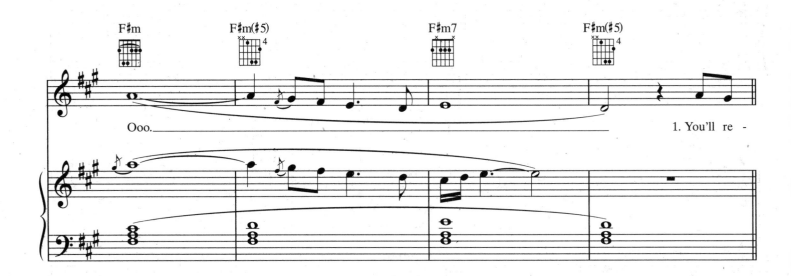

Ooo.                                                                1. You'll re -

**Slowly, poco rubato** ♩ = 80

*Verse 1:*

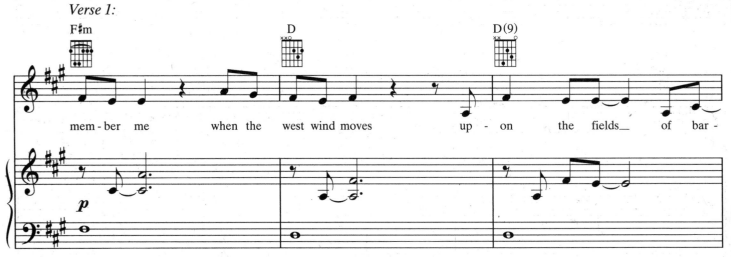

mem - ber me      when the   west wind moves      up - on    the   fields___  of   bar -

**A little faster**

**Moderately slow** ♩ = 92

*Verse 3:*

18

# WHEN YOU BELIEVE

(from *The Prince of Egypt*)

Words and Music by
STEPHEN SCHWARTZ

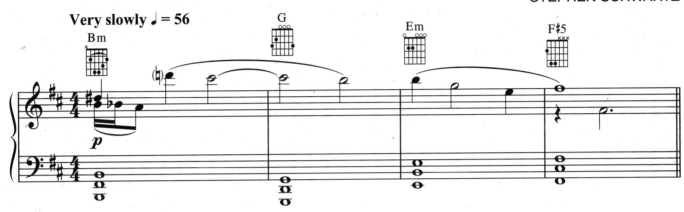

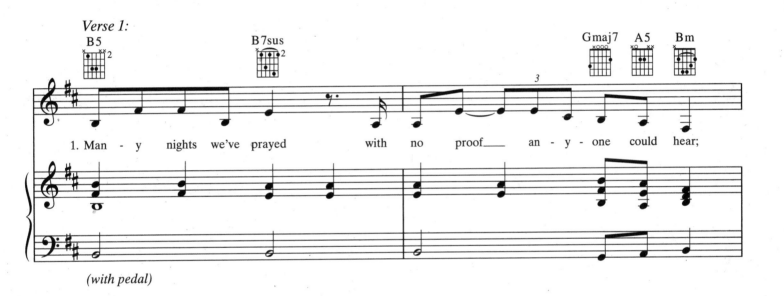

1. Man-y nights we've prayed with no proof__ an-y-one could hear;

(with pedal)

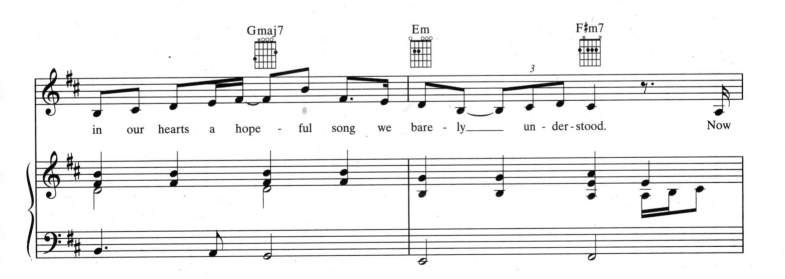

in our hearts a hope-ful song we bare-ly__ un-der-stood. Now

When You Believe - 7 - 1
34439

# THE COAST OF GALIÇIA

Traditional
*Arranged by DAVID DOWNES*

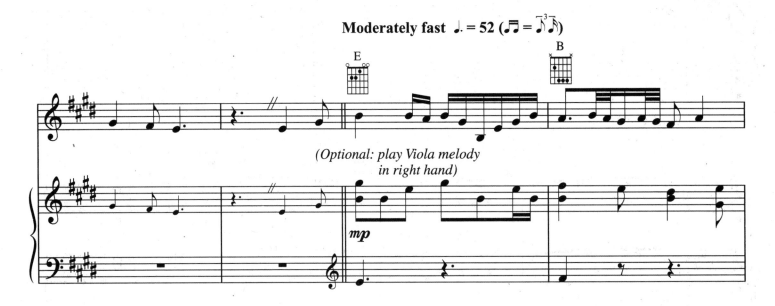

(Optional: play Viola melody
in right hand)

# THE NEW GROUND

Music by
DAVID DOWNES

**Slowly, with feeling** ♩ = 66

The New Ground - 2 - 1
34439

(with pedal)

cresc.

*Segue to "Isle of Hope, Isle of Tears"*

# ISLE OF HOPE, ISLE OF TEARS

Words and Music by
BRENDAN GRAHAM

# NON C'È PIÙ

Lyrics by
**BARRY MCCREA** and
**CAITRÍONA NÍ DHUBHGHAILL**

Music by **ANTONIN DVORÁK**
*Arranged by* DAVID DOWNES

cor - ri sem - pre giù. Quan - do-tro - vi il ma - re fiu - me non c'è più.

Ooh._____

Wave of blue, long a - go, noth - ing but a stream. Rush - ing through moun - tain dew

On - da, ca - di__ per__ un sog -

to the sea's gold gleam. Noth - ing but a stream towards the o - cean dream.

no.

# TRUE COLOURS

Words and Music by
BILLY STEINBERG and TOM KELLY

Verse 2:

2. So, sad eyes, take cour-age now___ and

# GALWAY BAY

Words and Music by
DR. ARTHUR COLAHAN

cab - in        and watch the bare - foot gos-soons at    their play.

(Bagpipes)                    (Vocal joins Bagpipes with "ooh.")

*a tempo*

*Verse 3:*

3. For the breez - es blow-ing o'er__ the sea__ from

*rit.*        *mf* *a tempo*

# GOODNIGHT MY ANGEL

Words and Music by
BILLY JOEL

# O, AMERICA!

Words and Music by
BRENDAN GRAHAM and
WILLIAM JOSEPH

**Slowly, majestically** ♩ = 60

O, America! - 6 - 1
34439

# NÍL SÉ'N LÁ

Lyrics by
**BARRY MCCREA** and
**CAITRÍONA NÍ DHUBHGHAILL**

Traditional
*Arranged by DAVID DOWNES*

**Moderately** ♩ = 104

*4 measure percussion intro:*

Dum da___ do___ day___ a doh dum da___ do___ deh doy ee oy ee

un da___ do___ day___ a doh dum da___ do___ da die aye ee

um da___ do___ de doy ee oy ee um da___ do___ a do *ahhh.*

1. Chuaigh mé

*Verse:*

'steach i dteach a - réir___ is d'iarr mé cart ar bhean a' lean - na. 'Sí dúirt sí

Níl Sé'n Lá - 11 - 1
34439

liom, ní bhfaighidh tú deoir. Buail an bóthar is gabh a - bha - ile.

I came by a house last night and told the

wom - an I am stay-ing. I said to her, the moon is bright and my fid - dle's tuned for play -

ing.

(Solo Fiddle)

2. Tell me

that the night is long,___ tell me that the moon is glow - ing. Fill my

glass, I'll sing___ a song,___ and we'll start the mu - sic flow - ing. Nev - er

mind the ris - ing light, there's no sign of day___ or dawn - ing. In my

lá's ní bheigh go fóíll__ sol-as ard a-tá sa gheal - aigh.

*(Solo Fiddle)*

Fill the glass - es one more time__ and nev - er heed__ the emp - ty bot - tle.

Turn the wa - ter in - to wine___ and turn the par - ty up full throt-tle!

(Solo Fiddle)

3. Don't go

*Verse:*

out in to the cold___ where the wind and rain are blow--ing. For the

that the moon is glow - ing. Fill my glass, I'll sing_ my song,_ and we'll

keep the mu - sic stream - ing un - til all the songs_ are sung! Níl sé'n

*Chorus:*

lá, níl a ghrá,_ níl sé'n lá, ná baol ar mai - din. Níl sé'n

lá's ní bheigh go fóill_ sol - as ard_ a - tá sa gheal - aigh. Níl sé'n

# THE LOST ROSE FANTASIA

Music by
DAVID DOWNES

(with pedal)

**Slowly, con rubato** ♩ = 66

**Solo Violin:**

The Lost Rose Fantasia - 3 - 1
34439

**Much slower**

# THE MOON'S A HARSH MISTRESS

Words and Music by
JIMMY WEBB

The Moon's a Harsh Mistress - 5 - 1
34439

# YOU'LL BE IN MY HEART

(from Walt Disney Pictures' *Tarzan*™)

Words and Music by
PHIL COLLINS

**Moderately, with freedom** ♩ = 92

*Verse 1:*

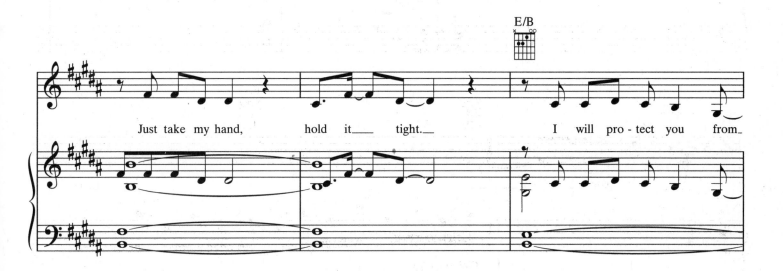

You'll Be in My Heart - 7 - 1
34439

# MY LAGAN LOVE

Traditional
*Arranged by DAVID DOWNES*

My Lagan Love - 4 - 1
34439

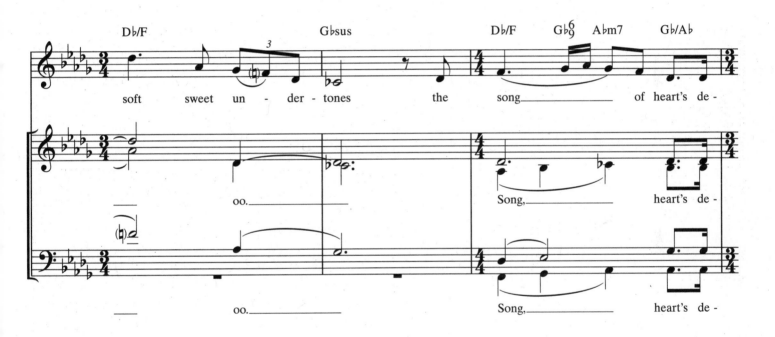

# AMAZING GRACE

Traditional
*Arranged by DAVID DOWNES*

(with pedal)

Lisa:

A -

# SLUMBER MY DARLING/THE MASON'S APRON

Traditional
*Arranged by DAVID DOWNES
and MAIREAD NESBITT*

**Slowly, freely (♪ = 96)**

*"Slumber My Darling"*

N.C.

(Solo Fiddle)

(with pedal)

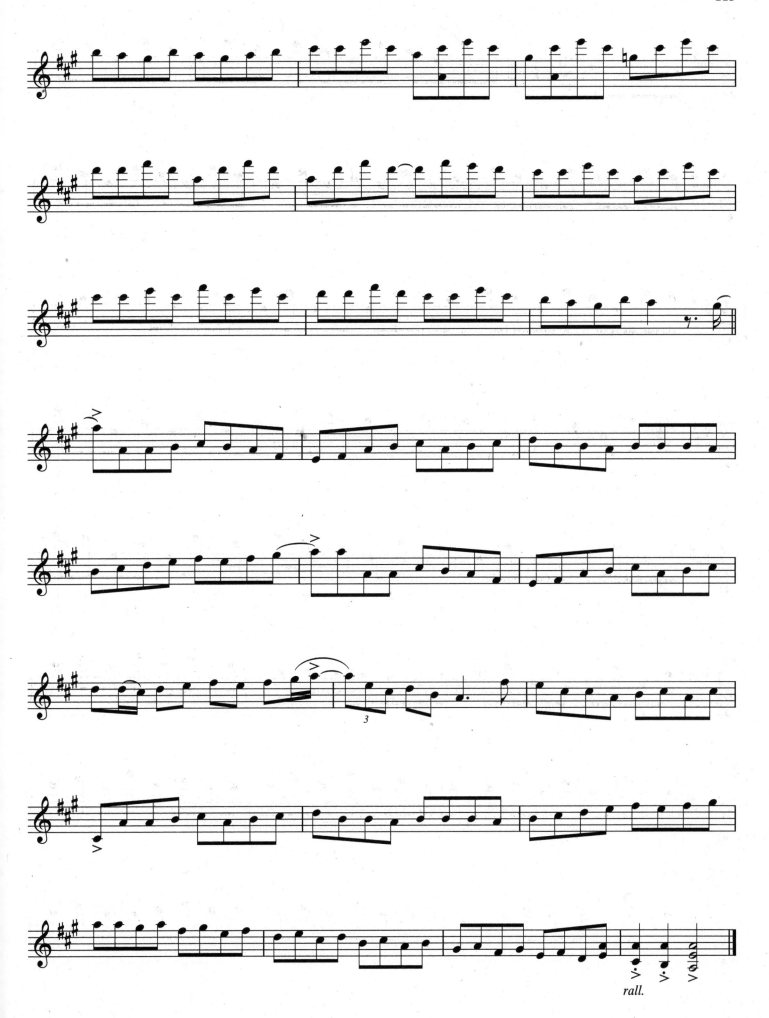

Slumber My Darling/The Mason's Apron - 6 - 6
34439

# DANNY BOY

Traditional
*Arranged by DAVID DOWNES*

**Slowly, freely (♩ = 63)**

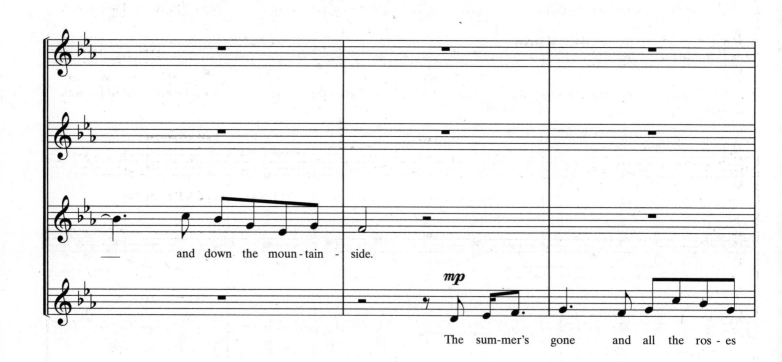

Danny Boy - 4 - 1
34439

# PIE JESU
## (from *Requiem*)

Traditional
*Arranged by* ANDREW LLOYD WEBBER

**Andante (freely and flowing)** ♩ = 48

(Violin solo)

*p*

(with pedal)

Pi - e Je - su,___ pi - e Je - su,___ pi - e Je - su,___ pi - e Je - su. Qui tol - lis pec - ca - ta mun - di. Do - na e - is re - qui - em, do - na e - is

# YOU RAISE ME UP

Words and Music by
ROLF LOVLAND and BRENDAN GRAHAM

You Raise Me Up - 5 - 1
34439

*Chorus:*

# FINALE/MO GHILE MEAR

Finale: Composed by DAVID DOWNES
*Mo Ghile Mear:* Traditional
*Arranged by DAVID DOWNES,*
*BARRY MCCREA and*
*CAITRÍONA NÍ DHUBHGHAILL*

**Brightly, crisp and rhythmic** ♩. = 138

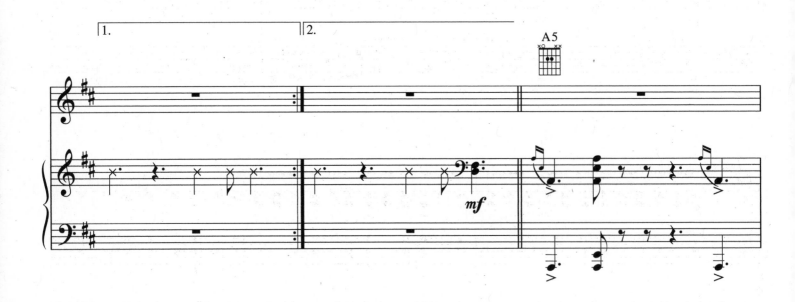

Finale/Mo Ghile Mear - 14 - 1
34439

128

Finale/Mo Ghile Mear - 14 - 3
34439

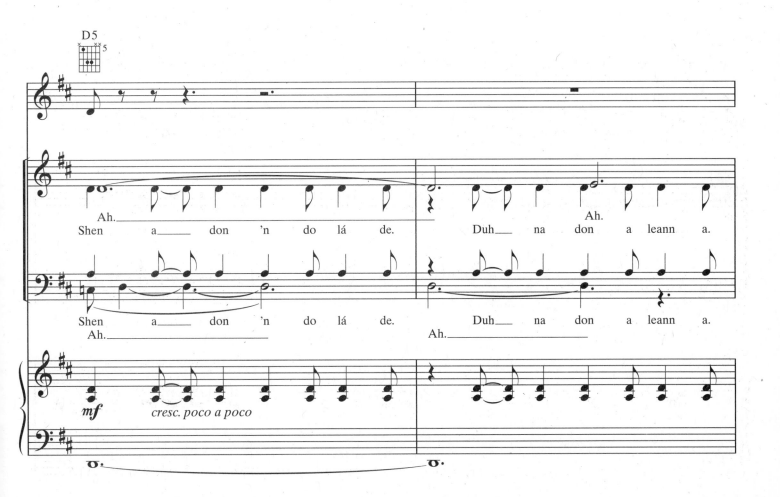

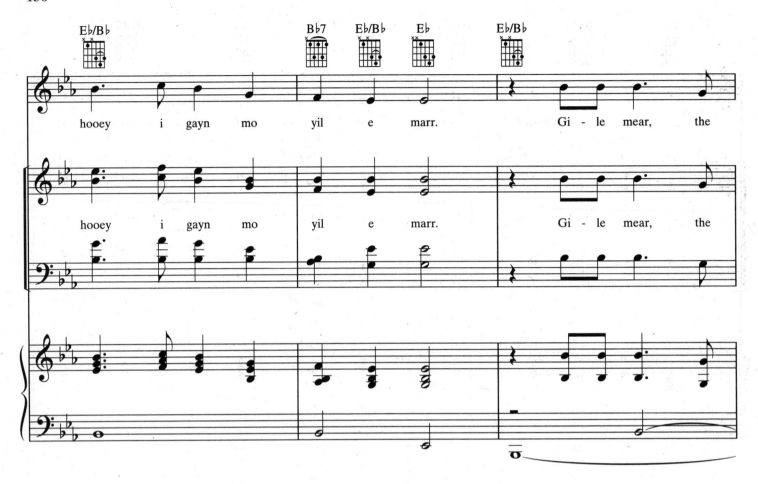

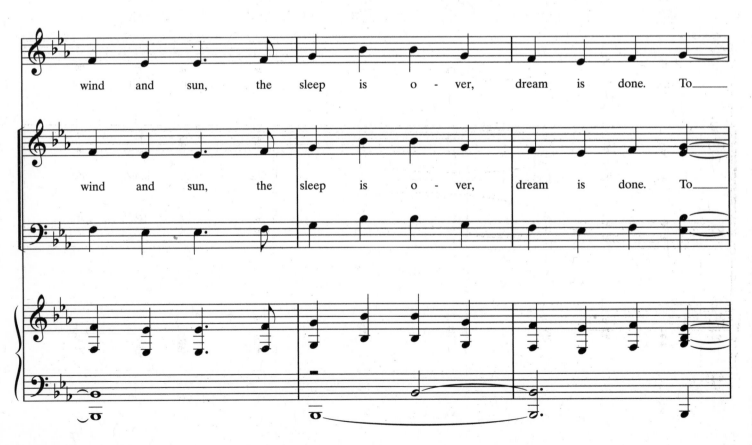

138

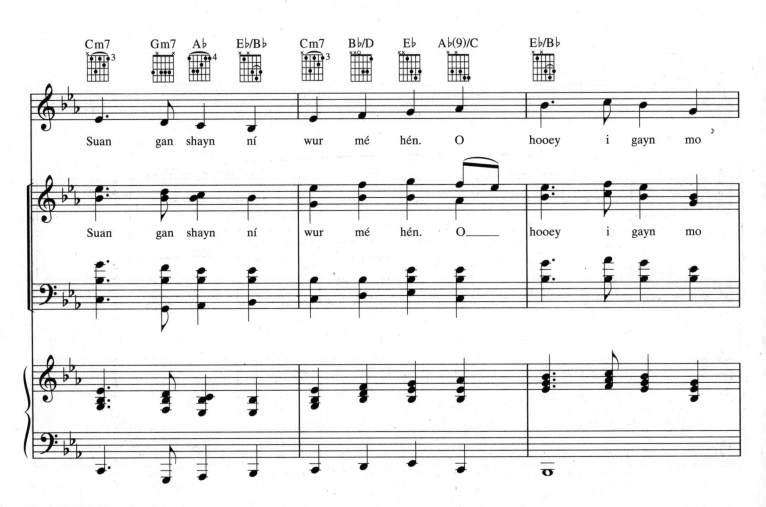

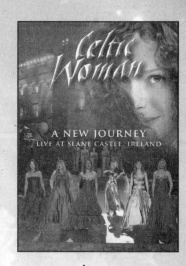

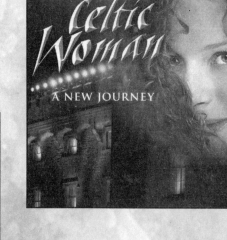

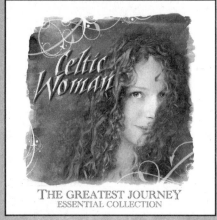

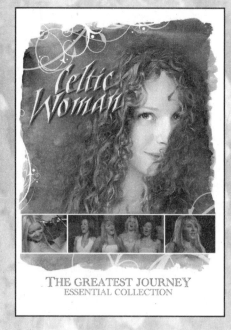

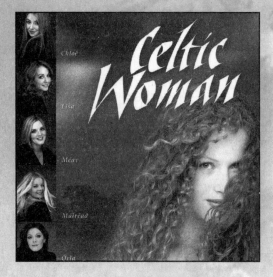